# .CLASSICS.
## *Illustrated*®

# William Shakespeare
# MACBETH

essay by
## Karen Karbiener
## Columbia University

ACCLAIM BOOKS
STUDY GUIDE

Macbeth

art by Alex Blum
adaptation by Lorenz Graham

*For Classics Illustrated Study Guides*
computer recoloring by VanHook Studios
editor: Madeleine Robins
assistant editor: Gregg Sanderson
design: Scott Friedlander

Dale-Chall R.L.  7.9

ISBN 1-57840-014-7

Acclaim Books, New York, NY
Printed in the United States

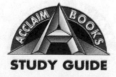

**STUDY GUIDE**

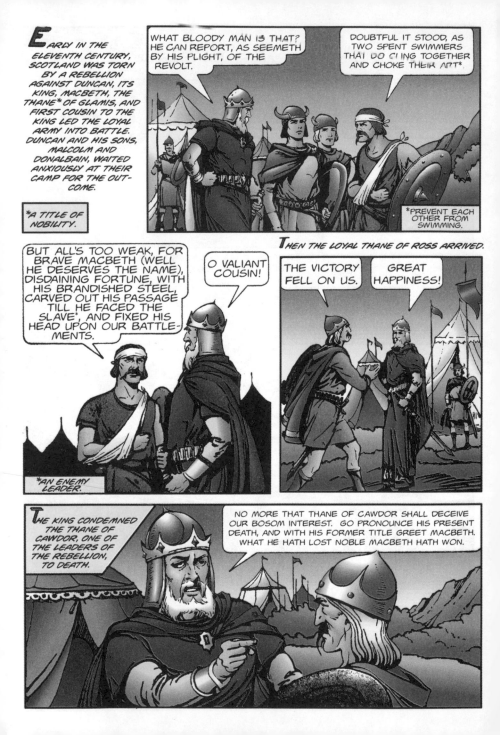

**AT** INVERNESS, MACBETH'S CASTLE, LADY MACBETH RECEIVED A LETTER FROM HER HUSBAND TELLING HER OF HIS NEW HONORS AND OF THE WITCHES' PROPHECIES. COLD AND CUNNING, LADY MACBETH, LIKE HER HUSBAND, KNEW THAT MACBETH COULD ONLY BE KING IF DUNCAN WERE DEAD.

GLAMIS THOU ART, AND CAWDOR, AND SHALT BE WHAT THOU ARE PROMISED. YET DO I FEAR THY NATURE. IT IS TOO FULL O' THE MILK OF HUMAN KINDNESS TO CATCH THE NEAREST WAY. HIE THEE HITHER, THAT I MAY POUR MY SPIRITS IN THINE EAR.

**A** MESSENGER THEN ENTERED.

THE KING COMES HERE TONIGHT.

THE RAVEN HIMSELF IS HOARSE THAT CROAKS THE FATAL ENTRANCE OF DUNCAN UNDER MY BATTLEMENTS. COME, YOU THAT TEND ON MORTAL THOUGHTS, UNSEX ME HERE AND FILL ME, FROM THE CROWN TO THE TOE, TOP-FULL OF DIREST CRUELTY! COME, THICK NIGHT, AND PALL* THEE IN THE DUNNEST** SMOKE OF HELL, THAT MY KEEN KNIFE SEE NOT THE WOUND IT MAKES, NOR HEAVEN PEEP THROUGH THE BLANKET OF THE DARK TO CRY "HOLD, HOLD!"

*COVER
**DARKEST

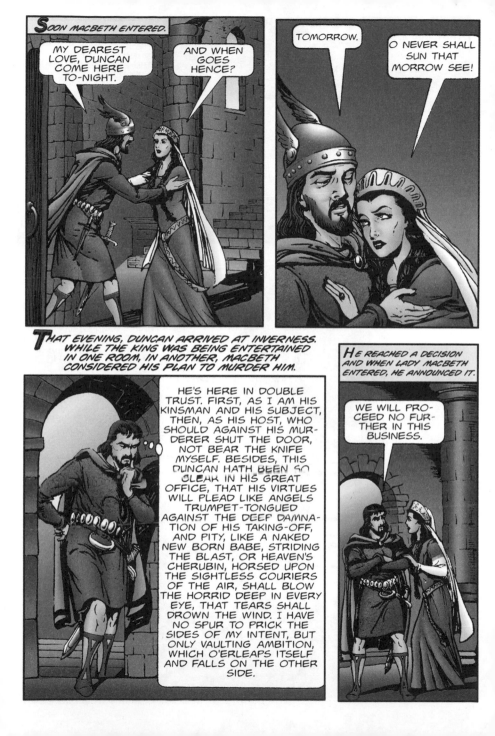

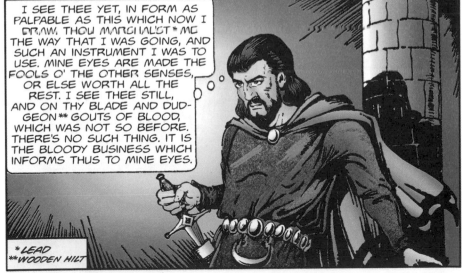

*LEAD
**WOODEN HILT

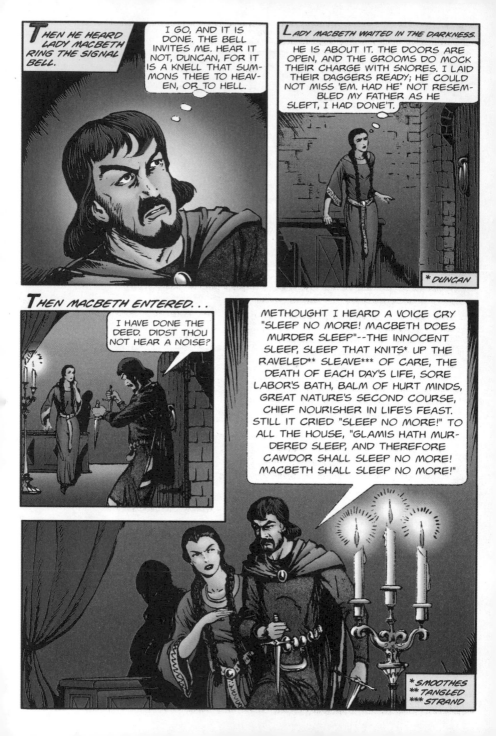

THE PORTER OPENED THE SOUTH ENTRY TO MACDUFF AND LENNOX.

IS THY MASTER STIRRING?

CALLED FROM HIS BEDROOM, MACBETH RECEIVED HIS GUESTS AND, AT MACDUFF'S REQUEST, DIRECTED HIM TO THE KING'S APARTMENT.

HE DID COMMAND ME TO CALL HIM; I HAVE ALMOST SLIPPED THE HOUR.

GOES THE KING HENCE TODAY?

HE DOES; HE DID APPOINT SO.

THE NIGHT HAS BEEN UNRULY. WHERE WE LAY, OUR CHIMNEYS WERE BLOWN DOWN, AND, AS THEY SAY, LAMENTINGS HEAR T' THE AIR, STRANGE SCREAMS OF DEATH, AND PROPHESYING, WITH ACCENTS TERRIBLE, OF DIRE COMBUSTION AND CONFUSED EVENTS NEW HATCHED TO THE WOEFUL TIME. THE OBSCURE BIRD* CLAMORED THE LIVELONG NIGHT. SOME SAY THE EARTH WAS FEVEROUS AND DID SHAKE.

'TWAS A ROUGH NIGHT.

*OWL

LATER, LADY MACBETH FOUND THE KING ALONE AND WORRIED.

HOW NOW, MY LORD! WHY DO YOU KEEP ALONE? THINGS WITHOUT ALL REMEDY SHOULD BE WITHOUT REGARD. WHAT'S DONE IS DONE.

WE HAVE SCORCHED* THE SNAKE, NOT KILLED IT. SHE'LL CLOSE AND BE HERSELF, WHILST OUR POOR MALICE REMAINS IN DANGER OF HER FORMER TOOTH. BUT LET THE FRAME OF THINGS DISJOINT, BOTH THE WORLDS SUFFER, ERE WE WILL EAT OUR MEAL IN FEAR AND SLEEP IN THE AFFLICTION OF THESE TERRIBLE DREAMS THAT SHAKE US NIGHTLY. BETTER BE WITH THE DEAD, WHOM WE, TO GAIN OUR PEACE, HAVE SENT TO PEACE, THAN ON THE TORTURE OF THE MIND TO LIE IN RESTLESS ECSTASY. DUNCAN IS IN HIS GRAVE, AFTER LIFE'S FITFUL FEVER HE SLEEPS WELL. TREASON HAS DONE HIS WORST. NOR STEEL, NOR POISON, MALICE DOMESTIC, FOREIGN LEVY, NOTHING, CAN TOUCH HIM FURTHER.

*SLASHED

I DO FORGET. DO NOT MUSE AT ME, MY MOST WORTHY FRIENDS. I HAVE A STRANGE INFIRMITY, WHICH IS NOTHING TO THOSE THAT KNOW ME. COME, LOVE AND HEALTH TO ALL! THEN I'LL SIT DOWN. GIVE ME SOME WINE, FILL FULL. I DRINK TO THE GENERAL JOY O' THE WHOLE TABLE, AND TO OUR DEAR FRIEND BANQUO, WHOM WE MISS. WOULD HE WERE HERE! TO ALL, AND HIM, WE THIRST, AND ALL TO ALL.

*BUT AS HE STARTED TO TAKE HIS SEAT, AGAIN HE SAW THE FORM OF THE MURDERED BANQUO.*

AVAUNT AND QUIT MY SIGHT! LET THE EARTH HIDE THEE! THY BONES ARE MARROWLESS, THY BLOOD IS COLD; THOU HAST NO SPECULATION IN THOSE EYES WHICH THOU DOST GLARE WITH!

I PRAY YOU, SPEAK NOT. HE GROWS WORSE AND WORSE. AT ONCE, GOOD NIGHT. STAND NOT UPON THE ORDER OF YOUR GOING, BUT GO AT ONCE.

*AFTER THE DEPARTURE OF THE GUESTS...*

YOU HAVE DISPLACED THE MIRTH, BROKE THE GOOD MEETING WITH MOST ADMIRED DISORDER.

IT WILL HAVE BLOOD, THEY SAY, BLOOD WILL HAVE BLOOD.

I WILL TO-MORROW TO THE WEIRD SISTERS. MORE SHALL THEY SPEAK, FOR NOW I AM BENT TO KNOW, BY THE WORST MEANS, THE WORST, FOR MINE OWN GOOD ALL CAUSES SHALL GIVE WAY. I AM IN BLOOD STEPPED IN SO FAR THAT SHOULD I WADE NO MORE, RETURNING WERE AS TEDIOUS AS GO O'ER.

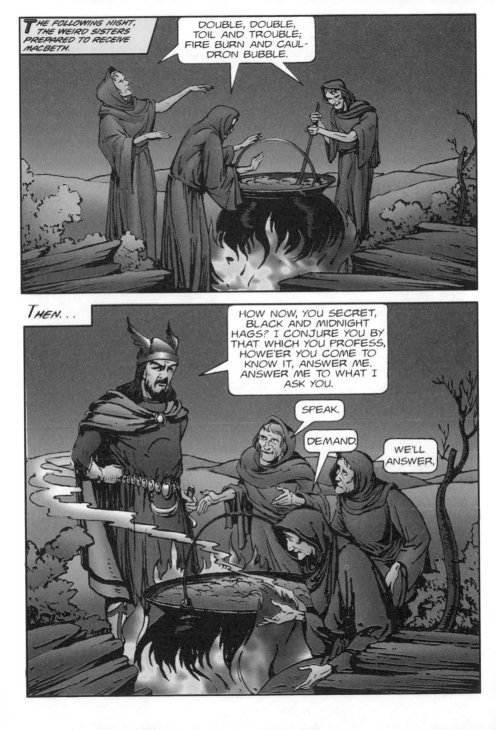

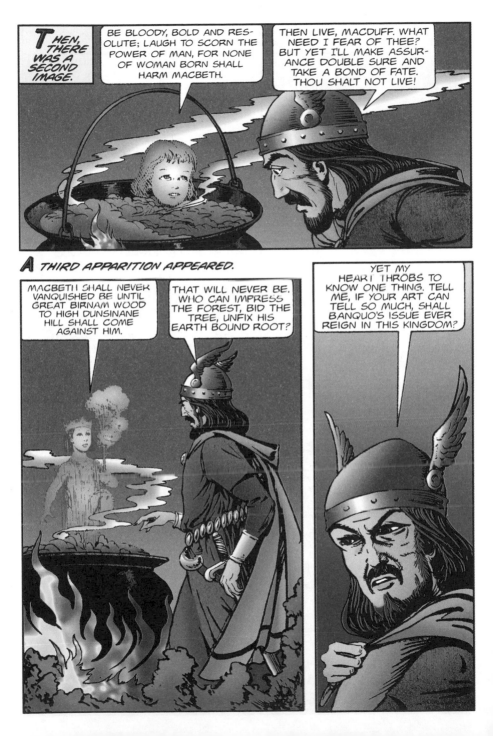

* MACDUFF

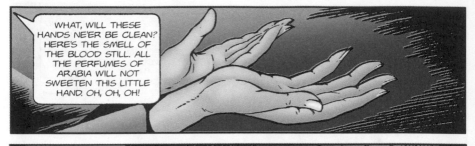

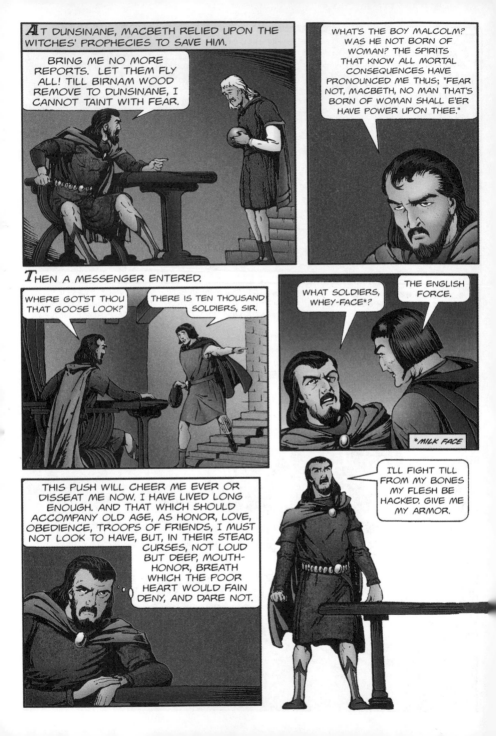

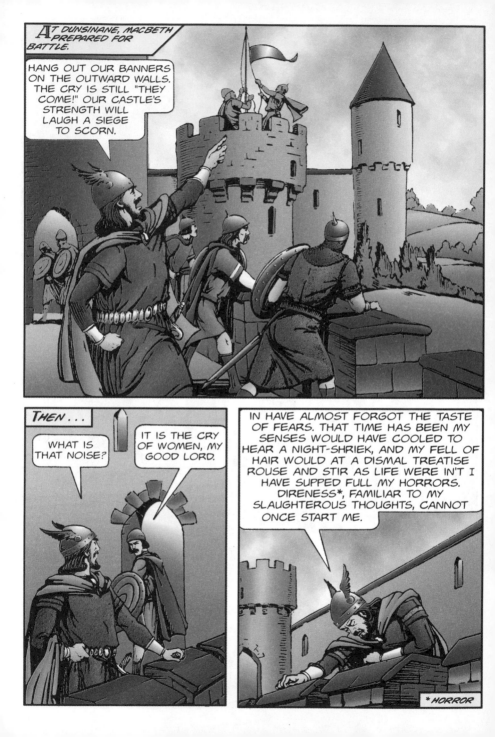

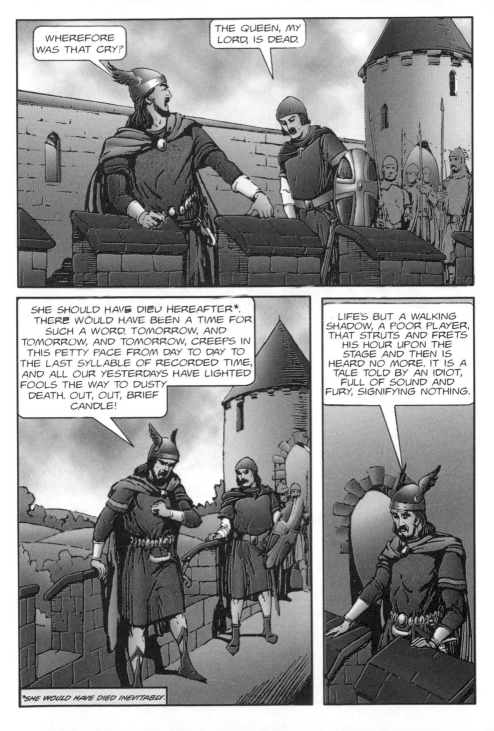

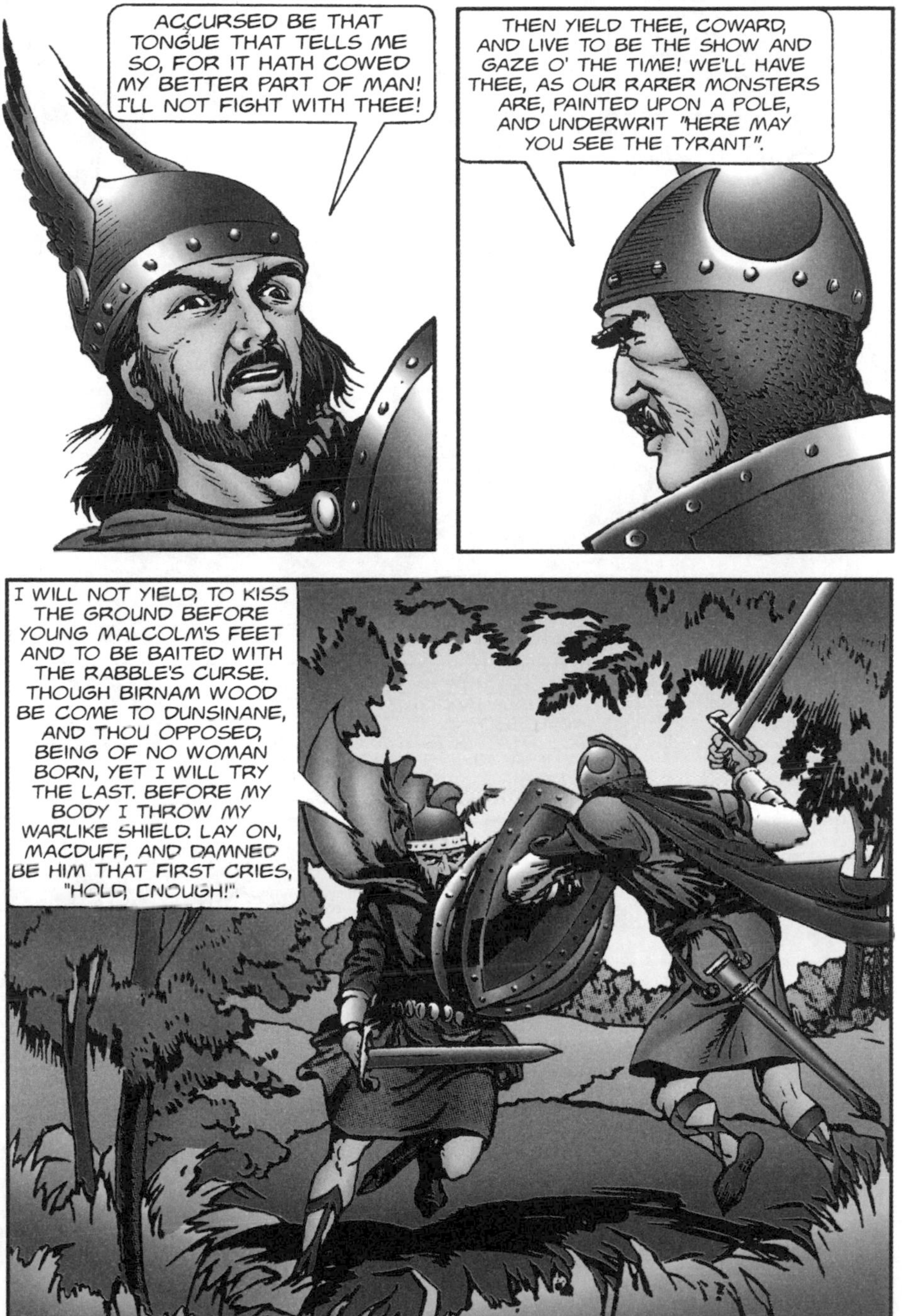
ACCURSED BE THAT TONGUE THAT TELLS ME SO, FOR IT HATH COWED MY BETTER PART OF MAN! I'LL NOT FIGHT WITH THEE!
THEN YIELD THEE, COWARD, AND LIVE TO BE THE SHOW AND GAZE O' THE TIME! WE'LL HAVE THEE, AS OUR RARER MONSTERS ARE, PAINTED UPON A POLE, AND UNDERWRIT "HERE MAY YOU SEE THE TYRANT".
I WILL NOT YIELD, TO KISS THE GROUND BEFORE YOUNG MALCOLM'S FEET AND TO BE BAITED WITH THE RABBLE'S CURSE. THOUGH BIRNAM WOOD BE COME TO DUNSINANE, AND THOU OPPOSED, BEING OF NO WOMAN BORN, YET I WILL TRY THE LAST. BEFORE MY BODY I THROW MY WARLIKE SHIELD. LAY ON, MACDUFF, AND DAMNED BE HIM THAT FIRST CRIES, "HOLD, ENOUGH!".

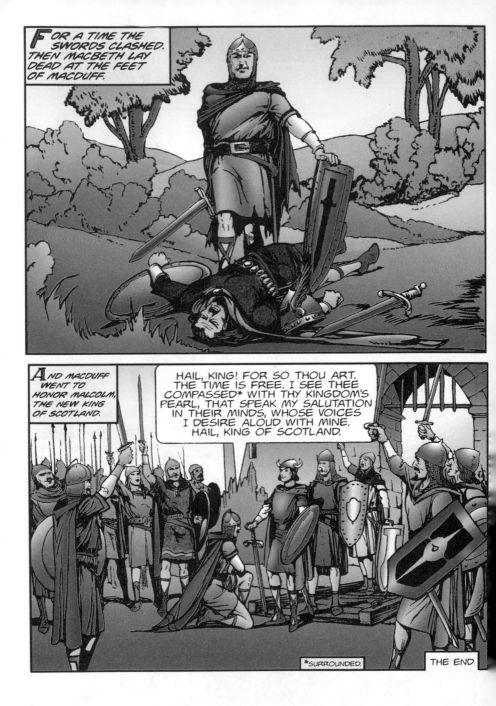

FOR A TIME THE SWORDS CLASHED. THEN MACBETH LAY DEAD AT THE FEET OF MACDUFF.

AND MACDUFF WENT TO HONOR MALCOLM, THE NEW KING OF SCOTLAND.

HAIL, KING! FOR SO THOU ART. THE TIME IS FREE. I SEE THEE COMPASSED* WITH THY KINGDOM'S PEARL, THAT SPEAK MY SALUTATION IN THEIR MINDS, WHOSE VOICES I DESIRE ALOUD WITH MINE. HAIL, KING OF SCOTLAND.

*SURROUNDED.

THE END

# MACBETH
## WILLIAM SHAKESPEARE

Though Shakespeare's works have been analyzed and re-analyzed for centuries, his life remains shrouded in mystery. No biography of Shakespeare was attempted until over a century after his death, and there's very little documentation about the events of his life. Until the 18th-century, William Shakespeare was more a myth than a man—a character as wild as any in his own plays. There were tales of the butcher's eccentric son who delivered eloquent speeches as calves were being slaughtered; this was the lawless rascal who was caught poaching deer; this was the party animal who contracted a fever and died from drinking too much. In the 19th-century, partially in response to these legends of a disreputable Shakespeare, arguments developed that such a man could not have written the plays that bear his name. Suggestions of the identity of the real author included Queen Elizabeth, Sir Francis Bacon, and Christopher Marlowe.

We may want to believe that these plays must have been written by an aristo-

crat, a university graduate, or an undisciplined, misunderstood genius, but the fact remains that they were composed by a commoner from a market town with a good grammar school education, who took in life's experiences on London's streets and stages. Certainly, many intriguing questions remain about Shakespeare the man, about things like his sexual preferences and his reasons for entering the theater in the first place. But at the center of the Shakespeare mystery is Will himself: an ordinary guy with extraordinary talent.

In 1564, Shakespeare was born in the prosperous and picturesque town of Stratford-on-Avon, in the heart of rural England. His mother, Mary Arden, was related to a wealthy family holding large properties in the nearby countryside; his father, a leather worker, became one of Stratford's leading citizens, serving on the town council and even as mayor during William's infancy. Because of his father's position in town politics, William was entitled to free tuition at the local grammar school. Since he never went on to university, it was either at

the grammar school or on his own that Shakespeare established the solid basis in classical literature he relied on for his dramas.

Where Shakespeare gathered his knowledge of human nature and street smarts is less evident. We know he was married in 1582 to Anne Hathaway, who was eight years his senior; six months later, the oldest of their three children was born in Stratford. Where he was and what he was doing for the next ten years is uncertain, but by 1592 he was a published poet and had achieved some fame in London as both an  actor and a playwright. As a matter of fact, he was verbally attacked that year by the playwright Robert Greene, who was jealous of the young writer competing so successfully with university-educated dramatists like himself.

As the plague raged through London in 1592 and 1593, theaters shut their doors, and Shakespeare concentrated on writing poetry. But when theaters reopened late in 1594, records show him to be a leading member of the Lord Chamberlain's Men. It was this company of actors, later renamed the King's Men, for whom he would be a principal actor, dramatist, and shareholder for the rest of his career.

This career, which spanned about twenty years, gave the world some of its greatest dramas and brought Shakespeare much worldly fortune. The popularity of his plays enabled him to buy one of the largest houses in Stratford by 1597; he could now call himself a gentleman, despite his connections with the theater. In 1599, Shakespeare's company built a theater for themselves across the river from London, and named it the Globe. The plays that are considered by many to be Shakespeare's major tragedies (*Hamlet*, *Othello*, *King Lear*, and *Macbeth*) were written while the company was resident in this theater. The company took over Blackfriars theatre as a winter house in 1608.

Gradually, Shakespeare gave up acting for writing. By 1610, he retired to Stratford; he wrote very little after 1612, the year in which he probably finished *King Henry VIII* (during the play's run the next year, the Globe Theater caught fire and burned to the ground). Anticipating his death, Shakespeare drafted a will in which he left most of his estate to his eldest daughter's family. But his bloodline was not perpetuated beyond his grandchildren. Shakespeare's true descendants are his plays, and the countless works they have inspired.

# SEEING A SHOW, ELIZABETHAN STYLE

Theatre-going in Shakespeare's time wasn't the high-brow activity we may consider it today. Everyone went, from the lowest-born to the most noble. The "cheap seats" then were what we call the Orchestra Section nowadays—the area directly surrounding the stage, which stuck right out into the audience area. Shakespeare's theatre, The Globe, had no roof (which meant that plays were performed during the day, and in good weather, or not at all), and were usually built in a circle or octagon, with several tiers of balconies facing the stage. There was seating in the balconies, but the groundlings—the folks in the cheap seats—had to stand up...or sit on the edge of the stage. You brought your lunch to the play, maybe bought some ale or a pastry from a seller (who might be strolling through the theatre, yelling like a hot-dog vendor at a baseball game) and watched the show—or didn't. Groundlings talked to, yelled at, even got into fights with the players!

There were no curtains to hide stagehands while sets were changed (or actors hiding from wrathful groundlings!) and in fact very few sets were used. When the Chorus (a sort of on-stage narrator) speaks in prologue of "Fair Verona, where we set our scene," or tells the audience

*"Think, when we talk of horses,*
*    that you see them*
*Printing their proud hoofs i' the*
*    receiving earth.*
*For 'tis your thoughts that now*
*    must deck our kings*
*Carry them here and there,*
*    jumping o'er times..."*

at the beginning of Shakespeare's history play *Henry V*, it was acknowledging that audience's imagination regularly supplied the settings the theatre itself could not.

Interior of the Swan Theatre.
From a drawing by Johannes de Witt (1596).

**Macbeth:** Macbeth, Thane of Glamis at the beginning of the story, gains the title of Thane of Cawdor through his valorous deeds, and King of Scotland through wicked acts of murder. From the very first scene, we know he is a bloody and ruthless warrior, though his behavior seems justified in the name of the benevolent King Duncan. When he kills in order to further himself instead of his liege, we begin to see Macbeth in a different light.

But is he really just a cold-blooded killer? His ambitious wife, preparing to convince Macbeth to kill Duncan, thinks that he is "too full of the milk of human kindness." Macbeth certainly seems to have a conscience: his troubling visions and his inability to sleep show that he is inwardly troubled, despite his terrifying actions. In Macbeth, Shakespeare has created an almost inhuman villain—but has allowed us a glimpse of his humanity.

**Lady Macbeth:** This famous villainess is Macbeth's "other half" not only in terms of name and relationship but in thought, word, and deed. It is she who convinces Macbeth to follow through on his plan to kill Duncan; it is she who calls upon the spirits of evil to aid them; it is she who completes the task when Macbeth is afraid. Macbeth's wife has often been judged as overly ambitious, but one must acknowledge that she does have her husband's best interests in mind, even in her most evil moments. And just like Macbeth, she presents herself to the world very differently from the way she may feel inside: she's not as tough as she looks. The first hint of her thin skin comes very soon in the play: though she lays out the daggers with which Macbeth will kill Duncan, she can't do the deed herself. And though she tells Macbeth that "a little water clears us of this deed," we see her later in the sleepwalking scene, unable to wash off imaginary spots from her hands. In the end, neither she nor her husband are able to enjoy their new power and prestige; the guilt—and the paranoia that

LATE THAT NIGHT, WHILE MACBETH AWAITED HIS WIFE'S SIGNAL THAT THE WAY WAS CLEAR, HE SAW BEFORE HIM THE IMAGE OF HIS INSTRUMENT.

IS THIS A DAGGER WHICH I SEE BEFORE ME, THE HANDLE TOWARD MY HAND? COME, LET ME CLUTCH THEE! I HAVE THEE NOT, AND YET I SEE THEE STILL. ART THOU NOT, FATAL VISION, SENSIBLE TO FEELING AS TO SIGHT? OR ART THOU BUT A DAGGER OF THE MIND, A FALSE CREATION, PROCEEDING FROM THE HEAT-OPPRESSED BRAIN?

accompanies it—proves to be too much for them.

Lady Macbeth is one of Shakespeare's most interesting female characters because of her seeming lack of femininity. When she asks the evil spirits to "unsex" her, so that she may be as cruel as possible she denies possessing any maternal instincts, and

THE RAVEN HIMSELF IS HOARSE THAT CROAKS THE FATAL ENTRANCE OF DUNCAN UNDER MY BATTLEMENTS. COME, YOU THAT TEND ON MORTAL THOUGHTS, UNSEX ME HERE AND FILL ME, FROM THE CROWN TO THE TOE, TOP-FULL OF DIREST CRUELTY! COME, THICK NIGHT, AND PALL* THEE IN THE DUNNEST** SMOKE OF HELL, THAT MY KEEN KNIFE SEE NOT THE WOUND IT MAKES, NOR HEAVEN PEEP THROUGH THE BLANKET OF THE DARK TO CRY "HOLD, HOLD!"

*COVER **DARKEST

describes how she might murder her own child in gory detail. Her own husband tells her that her character is suitable for raising sons, when he asks her to "bring forth men-children only." But Lady Macbeth never has any children at all—which may, in fact, be the root of the Macbeths' problems. Without an heir, their struggle to hold what they have stolen—Scotland itself—becomes meaningless. There is no one to whom they can pass the crown; their grasp on the country is a sterile stranglehold.

**Banquo:** "Lesser than Macbeth and greater," as the witches proclaim him, Banquo starts out as Macbeth's equal: they are close friends, and are both commanders in Duncan's army. But Banquo is a different

THE WITCHES' POWER BROUGHT BEFORE MACBETH THE VISION OF EIGHT KINGS, ALL DESCENDANTS OF BANQUO. THEY APPEARED ONE BY ONE, FOLLOWED BY BANQUO.

THOU ART TOO LIKE THE SPIRIT OF BANQUO DOWN! THY CROWN DOES SEAR MINE EYEBALLS. AND THY HAIR, THOU OTHER GOLD BOUND BROW, IS LIKE THE FIRST. A THIRD IS LIKE THE FORMER, FILTHY HAGS! WHY DO YOU SHOW ME THIS? A FOURTH! START, EYES! WHAT WILL THE LINE STRETCH OUT TO THE CRACK OF DOOM? ANOTHER YET! A SEVENTH! I'LL SEE NO MORE. AND YET THE EIGHTH APPEARS, WHO BEARS A GLASS WHICH SHOWS ME MANY MORE. HORRIBLE SIGHT! NOW I SEE 'TIS TRUE, FOR THE BLOOD-BOLTERED* BANQUO SMILES UPON ME AND POINTS AT THEM FOR HIS.

*HAIR MATTED WITH BLOOD

sort of person from Macbeth: he is a family man, and though he is well loved by the king he does not concentrate his energies on furthering his political career. Banquo does not act on the witches' predictions, but he becomes suspicious that Macbeth is engaging in foul play to speed along the witches' prophecy. And when he is murdered by Macbeth because he is in the way and knows too much, he comes back to haunt his friend as a ghost. (See previous page.)

Banquo also lives on in his son, Fleance, who manages to avoid being killed by Macbeth's hit men. Macbeth knows that this will be a problem; speaking of Fleance, he notes that "the worm that's fled hath nature that in time will venom breed." Indeed, the witches predicted from the beginning that Banquo's heirs would be kings. Why Macbeth does not pursue and try to kill Fleance is a mystery; perhaps Banquo's ghost conjures up unbearable guilt in Macbeth. But in the end, even as Malcolm is crowned the new king of Scotland, we realize that the witches' prophecy about Banquo's heirs will eventually be fulfilled; Banquo's descendant, England's King James I, is living and actual proof.

**Duncan:** Duncan is the King of Scotland before Macbeth murders him and assumes his title. Though he is only part of the story's action for a few scenes, he plays an important symbolic role. Duncan is a gentle, paternal figure for his Scottish subjects, and most pointedly for the Macbeths: Lady Macbeth thinks that he resembles her own father, and Macbeth recognizes him as a model of virtue and benevolence. Under Duncan's rule, Scotland is healthy and thriving.

So when Macbeth kills Duncan, he is in effect not only killing his "father" but Scotland's as well. Macbeth's character is permanently blackened by this act, and Scotland is plunged into a sterile darkness for the duration of Macbeth's reign.

**The Witches:** The fact that *Macbeth* begins with the three witches, or Weird Sisters, is significant because they turn out to be the ruling forces of the story. These are no cackling old women, but supernatural beings—great pow-

# The History of *Macbeth*

There was, in fact, a real Macbeth. He reigned in Scotland from 1034 to 1057; he actually did murder his predecessor, Duncan I, and was in turn killed by his successor, Duncan's son Malcolm III. Shakespeare's main source for his retelling of Macbeth's story was a book he also consulted for some of his history plays: Raphael Holinshed's Chronicles of England, Scotland, and Ireland (1587), the first authoritative and continuous account of the whole of English history. In this book, Shakespeare found a violent history of eleventh century Scotland—slaughters of armies and innocent families, assassinations of kings, and the execution of rebels.

Some time in the year 1606, Shakespeare sat down and wrote out his version of Macbeth's story, which would turn out to be the last of his four "great tragedies." Probably that same year, Shakespeare's *Macbeth* was performed for the first time in the presence of the royal court. The first record of the play's performance in a popular theater was noted by Dr. Simon Forman, an astrologist who claimed he saw *Macbeth* performed at the Globe Theater in 1611.

Why was Shakespeare interested in writing a play about this particular king, at this particular time in his career? He was actually riding a trend: in 1603, James VI of

Scotland became King James of England. Suddenly, London was flooded with Scots and interested in all things Scottish. Clearly, a play about Scotland was a smart business move.

Shakespeare had even more motivation to write a play about Macbeth. Only a few weeks after James I was crowned King of England, he selected Shakespeare and eight other actors and named them the King's Players. Under his patronage, Shakespeare and his company thrived in the London literary scene. A great way to show his appreciation to his patron was to write a play not only involving James I's beloved Scotland, but his personal Scottish heritage: the king was in reality an descendant of Banquo, a character closely associated with Macbeth in both fact and Shakespeare's fiction.

King James' familial ties with Banquo explain why Shakespeare altered some of the details of Holinshed's history. For example, in the Chronicles, Banquo plots with Macbeth to kill King Duncan; in his version of the story, Shakespeare makes Banquo an honorable man. This proved to be good politics as well as good playwriting on Shakespeare's part. By making Macbeth stand alone in the evildoings, he blackened Macbeth's guilt, and created one of his darkest, most intense villains.

ers or ministers of destiny. Their name comes from the Anglo-Saxon "wyrd," meaning fate; and indeed, their words shape Macbeth's fate, though we should realize that he has allowed them to do so.

The witches show up twice in the story. The first time they appear uninvited; significantly, Macbeth eagerly searches them out for the next meeting. His trust in them is the immediate cause of his downfall, and it may be surprising to us how unaware—even oblivious— Macbeth is of their foreboding aspects. Doesn't he notice their association with darkness, fog, and "filthy air"? Doesn't he see how they reverse moral values, as in their famous statement that "fair is foul, and foul is fair"? Isn't he wary of their sorcery, as any law-abiding citizen of a Christian land should be? In Shakespeare's time, and especially during the reign of King James I, witchcraft was a popular fixation; certainly, Macbeth's audience would have understood his association and acceptance of the witches as a premonition of evil to come.

**Macduff:** When Macduff appears late in the story, he seems to be an unlikely hero. We know that he left his wife and children in his castle in Scotland when he fled Macbeth's bloody rule. We also know, even before Macduff does, that he will pay dearly for his rashness: during his absence, Macbeth has his family murdered. Macduff strikes us as cowardly and irresponsible from the start. But Macduff turns out to be just the sort of man needed to

murder Macbeth, and to get Scotland out of its current stagnant state. He's the product of a cesarean birth, which was almost always fatal to the mother during the Renaissance; and just as he was rescued from a lifeless womb, so he will save Scotland from the sterility of Macbeth's rule. And while Macbeth might be a highly motivated tyrant, Macduff is fired by the wrath of a revengeful husband and father. When we see him wield the dagger that Macbeth had earlier envisioned and feared, we can see that Macbeth has met his match.

## The Plot

One of the most curious and striking aspects of the text of *Macbeth* is that it is one of Shakespeare's shortest plays, and by far the shortest of his great tragedies. Though Shakespeare sometimes limited the length of his comedies, he was a weaver of elaborate tales when it came to his histories and tragedies. These poetic worlds are often thickly peopled, and laden with subplots, twists, and complex character portraits.

In *Macbeth*, Shakespeare isn't interested in these things. There are only a few important characters besides Macbeth, and even these don't seem very well developed. Duncan and Banquo are killed before we learn too much about them, and Macduff seems rather predictable and two-dimensional in his role as the vigilante. Even Lady Macbeth fades in importance and power after her first infamous scene.

But it is the play's concentrated nature —its secure, swift direction and its lack of extra material—that is the key to its uniqueness in Shakespeare's canon. For the title character himself is fast-acting and utterly single-minded. Though he certainly is not a simple, straightforward villain, Macbeth could easily be categorized as a "doer," a man who must keep busy. It's his overwhelming and frightening need to act that keeps the play moving forward at such an accelerated pace; and when he runs out of things to do, the story must abruptly end.

From the time we are first introduced to Macbeth, we learn of his position as a "man of action": a messenger soldier comes to King Duncan and tells of Macbeth's victory over the rebel troops. In bloody detail, we learn of the unstoppable Macbeth, who slaughtered everyone in his way until he was able to behead the rebel leader. At this time, Macbeth is applauded as a decisive doer, and his murders are praised and rewarded as valorous acts. As will become too evident later, Macbeth is a product of a culture that values butchery, that equates manhood with the ability to kill.

RING THE ALARM BELL! BLOW, WIND! COME, WRACK*, AT LEAST WE'LL DIE WITH HARNESS ON OUR BACK!

*DESTRUCTION.

As a man of action, Macbeth cannot be subdued as easily as the rebel forces; he must continue to stir and act. The exception is his moment of hesitation before he commits his first vile act of murder: the killing of King Duncan, his friend, countryman, liege, and currently the guest in his home. Duncan has done nothing to deserve being put to death, and Macbeth knows it. For a brief moment the man of action is at war with his own "vaulting ambition."

As the fates would have it, Macbeth's voice of reason is drowned out by the call to action of his own wife. As Macbeth had at first been regarded a brave and noble soldier by his fellow Scots, Lady Macbeth seems to be an exemplary wife by the world's standards. She encourages and supports her husband in good wifely fashion; she does not undermine him; she sees, knows, and understands the terms of the world she lives in, and she accepts them. But like her husband, she doesn't know where to draw the line. She works herself into a frenzy, calling the forces of evil to her, and Macbeth's, aid. She has been sometimes compared with Eve from the Bible, since her communication with the forces of

METHOUGHT I HEARD A VOICE CRY "SLEEP NO MORE! MACBETH DOES MURDER SLEEP" -THE INNOCENT SLEEP, SLEEP THAT KNITS UP THE RAVELED* SLEEVE** OF CARE, THE DEATH OF EACH DAY'S LIFE, SORE LABOR'S BATH, BALM OF HURT MINDS, GREAT NATURE'S SECOND COURSE, CHIEF NOURISHER IN LIFE'S FEAST. STILL IT CRIED "SLEEP NO MORE!" TO ALL THE HOUSE, "GLAMIS HATH MURDERED SLEEP, AND THEREFORE CAWDOR SHALL SLEEP NO MORE! MACBETH SHALL SLEEP NO MORE!"

* SMOOTHES
** TANGLED
*** STRAND

# Reading Shakespeare's Verse

When reading Shakespearean verse it's okay to move your lips as you read! Shakespeare meant his lines to be spoken, and it's often by hearing, rather than reading, the words, that their true music and meaning come out. Almost all of Shakespeares plays were written in blank (unrhymed) iambic pentameter. That means, each line is made up of five "feet" with a particular kind of rhythm; in the case of an iamb, the rhythm of the foot is ba-BAII.

Thus, Macbeth declaims:

*Methought I heard a voice cry*
*"Sleep no more!*
*Macbeth does murder sleep"—*
   *the innocent sleep,*
*Sleep that knits up the raveled*
   *sleave of care,*
*The death of each day's life,*
   *sore labor's bath,*
*Balm of hurt minds, great*
   *nature's second course...*

It's interesting to know that when you hear a rhyme, it may have been a cue for stage-hands and cast members off stage to be ready for a scene change!

evil initiates the events that lead to the collapse of what could have been Macbeth's "paradise on earth"; but she also resembles the serpent herself, tempting and coaxing her husband into engaging in evil.

In her first and most important scene, Lady Macbeth seems to be less a lady, and more a Macbeth. She herself denies her sexuality, and asks the powers of darkness to "unsex" her so that she may be inhumanly cruel. And it is she that gives Macbeth his lessons of manhood, telling him that she would rather kill her own child than act as unmanly as he, as he backs down from his agreement to murder Duncan. Macbeth is soon inspired by her raw and ruthless energy; but while he becomes more defiant, she begins to lose the strength of her commitment. Though she would appear to be a natural doer like her husband, we learn that this role is too much for her. She is soon plagued with hesitations and doubts herself. The last time we see her, she is sleepwalking—an involuntary act that shows her lack of control and her total mental collapse. She's a far cry from the villainess who practically spit out fire with her words.

Macbeth is not fated to die from the pains of guilt as his wife does, though guilt plagues him in other ways.

First, he "loses control" of his eyes as he envisions the instrument of Duncan's murder: the dagger. Next, his ears begin to play tricks on him: he hears noises and knocking, and a voice tells him that he will "sleep no more." His mind eventually haunts him with

three-dimensional images that move and speak, like Banquo's ghost and the apparitions in the witches' cauldron. We're never sure whether these things are real or not; Shakespeare here seems to invite speculation about the mind's ability to create as well as destroy. But these sights and sounds give us a glimpse of the hellish confusion within Macbeth's soul, and add greatly to the dark, supernatural atmosphere of the story.

Indeed, few other Shakespearean plays besides *The Tempest* and *A Midsummer Night's Dream* contain so many supernatural references. We might want to remember that Shakespeare's patron at the time, James I, was a theologian and philosopher who was very concerned with explaining the nature and occurrence of evil. As a believer in witchcraft who had already condemned several women to death for practicing the "black arts," King James would have been immediately interested by *Macbeth*'s first scene, as well as the later appearance of the witches.

But the witches are clearly more than a gimmick put in the play to please the patron. Unlike the dagger or the knocking, they seem to be real; after all, Banquo sees them, and they do make accurate predictions. Shakespeare seems to have wanted these witches to really be there, visible to whom they wish, and endowed with powers appropriate to demons—but he also wanted them to represent temptation, not actual compulsion, to evil. The first time they appear before Macbeth, they subject him to the temptations he is least able to withstand, but they have no direct power over his free will; the only reason a second meeting takes place is because Macbeth has now chosen to search them out.

It's significant that, in the apparitions Macbeth envisions in the cauldron, two infants are central. Macbeth's state of childlessness is, of course, his big concern. He's haunted by the witches' earlier prediction that Banquo's children would carry the kingly lineage; with Banquo's son Fleance still alive, this was certainly a possibility. The first baby gives Macbeth a message that would seem to give him much hope: no man born of woman will kill Macbeth. Macbeth is reassured. But what he doesn't realize is that the bloody baby symbolizes Macduff, who was born "unnaturally," covered with blood from his mother's cesarean delivery. Perhaps Macduff's having been born "bloody" gives him that necessary edge over Macbeth, who only became "bloody" with time. The second babe in the vision gives Macbeth another apparently reassuring message: King Macbeth cannot be overthrown until a great forest known as Birnam Wood is moved to the hill outside Macbeth's castle. Macbeth should have noticed, however, that the babe bears a tree, which suggests the coming of Birnam Wood to Dunsinane; fur-

thermore, the child is healthy and crowned, perhaps representing a "natural" and organic line of succession—all the way to Shakespeare's patron, King James I.

Though he is comforted by the claims of the ghostly children, Macbeth remains a ruthless killer. His last murder is also his lowest action, and brings the play to its moral climax: he has Lady Macduff and her child murdered. What makes this act especially disturbing and pitiful is that Macbeth has bloodied the play's first and only domestic scene. In this play, whose women are "unsexed" and whose children are separated from their parents, a picture of mother and child together is a rare and heartwarming moment.

For a time the swords clashed. Then Macbeth lay dead at the feet of Macduff.

Macbeth's destruction of this family is symbolic of what happens when those in power have forgotten what they were supposed to protect in the first place. Macbeth has totally lost his judgment. But thankfully, the moral climax is also the play's moral turning point: the horror of it is enough to incite the only man capable of defeating Macbeth to action.

From the point Macbeth achieves the highest position guaranteed to him by the witches, time is no longer on his side. All the childless king can do is stall the future, but the cycle of days, seasons, and years constantly remind him of his own steady decay and eventual death. With the death of his wife, Macbeth's hopes for renewal or rebirth completely disappear.

Time may destroy Macbeth's hopes, but it also helps redeem the situation he created. The increasing suffering of the Macbeths may be thought of as caused by the pressure of the world of order as it slowly resumes its true shape. As usual in Shakespeare, evil, however great, burns itself out, and time is the servant of good. The play may have begun in darkness, but it ends in light—with power restored to its proper, natural place.

## Themes

### Ambition

*Macbeth* can, of course, be enjoyed simply as a very good story about a very evil man. But there are other ways of reading Shakespeare's drama, one of the most popular being as a moral tale about the power and problems of human ambition. "I have no spur to prick the sides of my intent, but vaulting ambition," concludes Macbeth, as he considers turning against people who have cared about him, and those he used to care about. Besides his desire for power and position, he has no reason to murder the benevolent King Duncan, his best friend Banquo, or the helpless wife and children of Macduff. Lady Macbeth, too, is motivated purely by her aspirations for her husband and herself. No one has given either of the

LATER, ALONE IN HIS CHAMBER, MACBETH ALSO REMEMBERED.

THERE IS NONE BUT HE WHOSE BEING I DO FEAR, AND UNDER HIM MY GENIUS IS REBUKED. THE SISTERS HAILED HIM FATHER TO A LINE OF KINGS. IF'T BE SO, FOR BANQUO'S ISSUE HAVE I FILED* MY MIND; FOR THEM THE GRACIOUS DUNCAN HAVE I MURDERED; TO MAKE THEM KINGS, THE SEED OF BANQUO KINGS! RATHER THAN SO, COME, FATE, INTO THE LIST, AND CHAMPION ME TO THE UTTERANCE **.

* DEFILED
** UTMOST

Macbeths cause to engage in evil acts, and yet they are willing to risk everything for possession of Scotland's crown.

Eventually we start to wonder why Macbeth and his wife are so driven by this worldly ambition. They have murdered their closest friends and innocent bystanders. Peaceful sleep becomes a distant memory. Their guilty minds begin to play tricks on both of them. They can't trust anyone, and nobody trusts them either. And how does ruling Scotland benefit them? Neither Macbeth nor Lady Macbeth seems to care especially about Scotland or the Scots as a people. Their rule has diminished the quality of life for the Scottish people and themselves. Additionally, they can only maintain power for so long;

without an heir, Macbeth's reign as king is measured by the relentless ticking of Time's clock. In short, Macbeth's ambition has destroyed his good name and his position. He seems to hate himself, from inside. Life has become meaningless; as he says, "it is a tale told by an idiot, full of sound and fury, signifying nothing."

And yet, Macbeth's passion for power and his instinct for self-assertion are so compelling that no inward misery persuades him to give up or repent. The only reason he loses out at all in the end is that someone else's ambition proves stronger than his own.

## Imagination

Macbeth's ambition is not the only thing that gets the better of him. He also possesses a very powerful imagination—or perhaps his imagination possesses him, at least when he is still in touch with his human side. Macbeth may not seem to be more imaginative than Banquo at first, since they both "see" the witches; the

Macbeths' plan to kill Duncan and thus gain the crown is also simple and straightforward, rather than creative. But when Macbeth's imagination is truly activated, he becomes vibrant and animated, full of life and feeling. His face betrays his true emotions, and he speaks straight from the heart. We see this behavior clearly when Macbeth envisions the dagger, hears the knocking, or reacts to the ghost of Banquo; in these instances, we have a window into Macbeth's troubled and complicated soul.

Something happens to Macbeth's powers of imagination towards the end of the story. He seems to trust too much in the words of the witches' apparitions. Instead of analyzing their predictions in an open, creative way, Macbeth takes as fact that "none of woman born shall harm Macbeth" and that he will never be defeated until "Great Birnam Wood to High Dunsinane Hill shall come against him." His lack of imagination is his downfall, and he is taken by complete surprise when a man of cesarean birth proves to be his mortal enemy, and when the rival army launches a surprise attack on Macbeth's castle by hiding behind branches from Birnam Wood.

How has Macbeth's active mind become so dulled? He gives us a clue when he reacts so mechanically to the sound of women crying at his wife's death. "I have almost forgot the taste of fears," Macbeth murmurs. "I have supped full with horrors. Direness, familiar to my slaughterous thoughts, cannot once start me." His imagination, once the register of his all-too-human emotions, has been overloaded and worn out by such atrocities as the murder of Macduff's family. And it is this sullen, hateful Macbeth—the Macbeth that seems more self-controlled and practical, rather than unrestrained and visionary— who will ultimately fail.

## Succession

The importance and naturalness of the flow of generations is another theme to be found in the pages of *Macbeth*. Shakespeare was probably inspired by the actual history of the rise to the throne of King James I, his patron. Queen Elizabeth I, who ruled England until 1603, was childless. Rumored to be incapable of bearing children, she even described herself as "barren stock." In a strange twist of fate, she had to allow James VI of Scotland to become her successor—even though he was the son of her cousin Mary, Queen of Scots, who had been beheaded by Queen Elizabeth's own decree. In a demonstration of the curse of unfruitfulness and the blessing reserved for those who carry on the race, Elizabeth became all but a memory to her people, and James VI became King James I of England.

The childless Macbeth can thus be directly compared to Queen Elizabeth: he may rule England, but his power is limited, sterile, and repressive. Only when the rightful, natural heirs gain control of the throne is happiness and prosperity restored in the kingdom. In this way, Banquo—who is, in historical reality, an ancestor of James I—resembles Mary, Queen of Scots: he suffers an untimely death but lives on

through his children's children. With a nod to the Bible, Shakespeare seems to preach that blessed, indeed, are those who are fruitful and multiply!

No one can say for certain that Macbeth desires to be childless; in fact, he bids his wife to "bring forth men-children only." A son

LADY MACBETH'S PLAN CONVINCED MACBETH.

BRING FORTH MEN-CHILDREN ONLY FOR THY UNDAUNTED METTLE* SHOULD COMPOSE NOTHING BUT MALES. AWAY, AND MOCK THE TIME WITH FAIREST SHOW; FALSE FACE MUST HIDE WHAT THE FALSE HEART DOTH KNOW.

*SUBSTANCE

and an heir would have dramatically changed the whole story; the Macbeths wouldn't have had to engage in such a fierce battle against time, and they wouldn't have had to face an inevitable end. So why doesn't the couple have any children?

It seems easiest to place the blame on Lady Macbeth, who asks evil spirits to "unsex" her. She certainly doesn't possess a mother's instinct; her description of what she would do to her baby, rather than live with Macbeth's uncertainty and lack of courage, is shockingly heartless.

But it couldn't have been her fault alone: Macbeth isn't much of a family man himself. He actually seems destined to break up families, rather than create them. Perhaps his inability to become a father is linked to his "robberies" of fathers from their children, or children from their fathers. The murder of his friend and patron King Duncan can be seen as parricide—the murder not only of Malcolm's father, but of the nation's as well. In killing Banquo, Macbeth leaves the boy Fleance fatherless. It seems only fitting that Macbeth meets his match in Macduff, an emotionally devastated father seeking revenge for the murder of his family.

OUT, DAMNED SPOT! OUT, I SAY!

## Study Questions

•What do you think this play says about the differences between permissible and impermissible violence? What are the moral differences between killing for one's country and killing for oneself?

•In what ways do the characters and actions of Macbeth and his wife parallel those of Adam and Eve in the story of Genesis? How does their world resemble a fallen Eden? What biblical characters might Shakespeare have been thinking of when he created the witches and King Duncan?

•Do you think that the witches have power over the future? Why or why not? What does your answer suggest about your own opinions concerning fate versus free will?

•In what ways is *Macbeth*'s ending not necessarily "happy" or satisfactory? Do you have any suggestions for a better one?

•Human ambition is both a natural survival technique and a deadly drive: discuss how Shakespeare's *Macbeth* supports this paradox.

•How does the possession or lack of imagination help or hurt other characters in *Macbeth*?

•Think of some examples of good and bad parenting that are suggested in the story of *Macbeth*. How can these tactics be used—for better or for worse—in other areas, such as war or politics?

# About the Essayist:

A doctoral candidate and Presidential Fellow of Columbia University, Karen Karbiener holds an MPhil from Columbia and an MA from Bryn Mawr College. She is currently an instructor in the Department of English at Columbia.